Alison Hawes

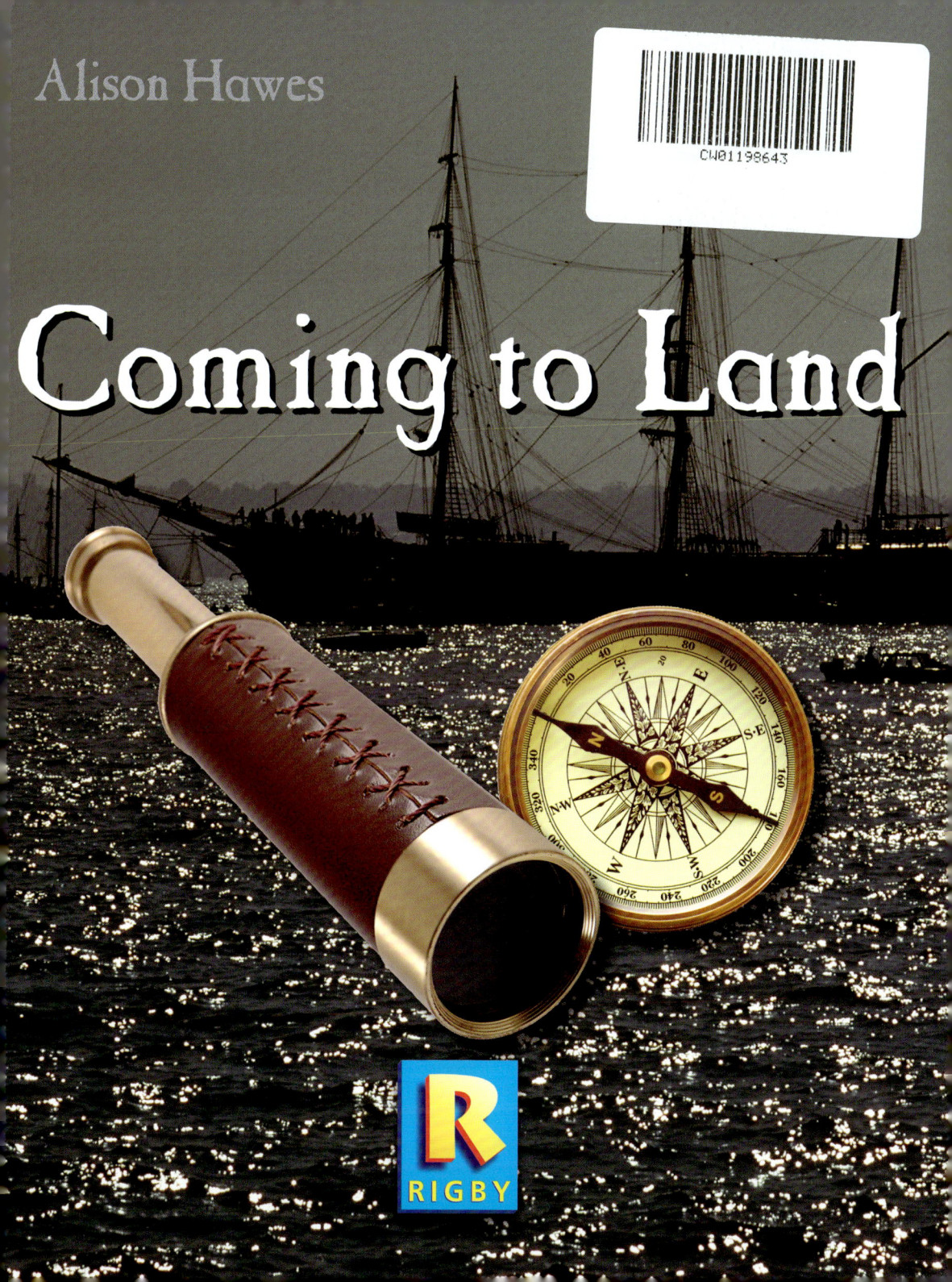

Coming to Land

Contents

Coming to land 4

Finding land 8

A safe landing 12

Islands 16

Desert islands 20

Picture glossary 24

Coming to land

Pirates spent a lot of time at sea.

But they spent time on land, too.

Pirates came to land to spend their money!

Meat and other food soon went rotten on the old pirate ships.

Food rotted in the sun.

Pirates came to land to get fresh food and drinking water.

There are often big storms at sea.

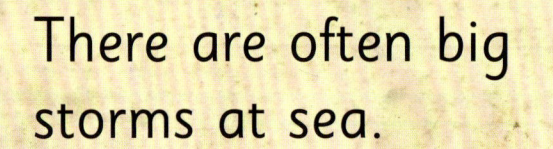

Pirates came to land to get away from a storm.

They also came to land to clean and mend their ships.

They also hid on land, from the people they robbed!

An island with lots of trees was a good place to hide.

Finding land

Pirates had lots of things to help them find land.

They had maps of the land and sea to look at.

They had telescopes to look through.

Telescopes helped them to spot land far away.

9

A pirate could spot land from the lookout.

The lookout was at the top of the tallest mast.

Pirates also used a compass to help them find land.

A compass showed the pirates which way the ship was sailing.

A safe landing

A pirate captain had to find a safe place to land.

He had to look out for rocks.

Rocks can smash holes in the bottom of a ship.

Lighthouses help ships to find land safely.

They warn ships of rocks and cliffs.

At night, a lighthouse shines a light out over the sea.

A harbour was a safe place for a pirate ship if there was a storm.

The harbour helped to keep a ship safe from strong winds and big waves.

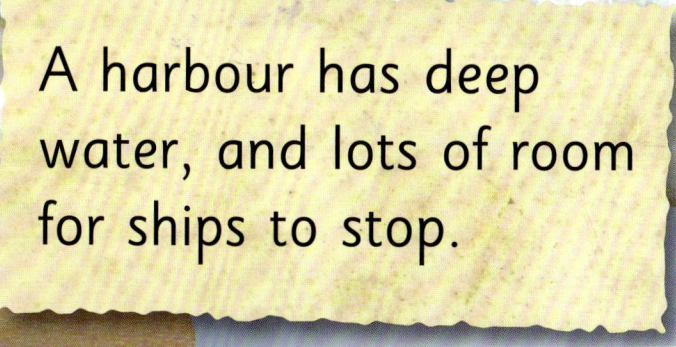

A harbour has deep water, and lots of room for ships to stop.

Pirates liked to drop anchor in a safe harbour, and go on shore.

A ship's anchor stops the ship floating away.

Islands

An island was a safe place to land, too.

It was sometimes a good place to hide too.

This island has lots of mountains to hide in.

This island was a good place for pirates, too.

It had lots of coconuts and fish for the pirates to eat.

This was also a good place for pirates to land.

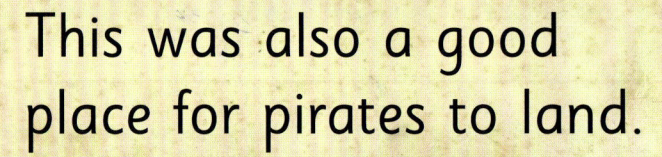

There was lots of fresh water here for them to drink.

Long ago, this island was a pirate island.

Lots of pirates landed here.

They found fruit, fish, animals and fresh water here.

Desert Islands

Desert islands are islands with no people on them.

Pirates were left on a desert island to punish them.

They had to find food and water quickly, to stay alive.

But not all desert islands have food and fresh water!

Sometimes pirates were shipwrecked on a desert island.

They built a big bonfire.

If they were lucky, a ship saw the fire and rescued them!

Picture glossary

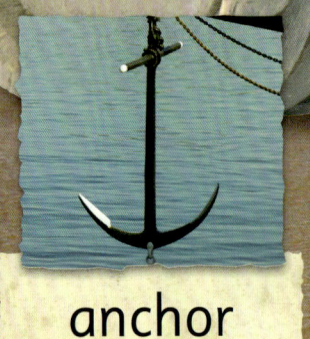

anchor	compass	lookout
harbour	island	lighthouse
map	telescope	shipwreck